What's This?

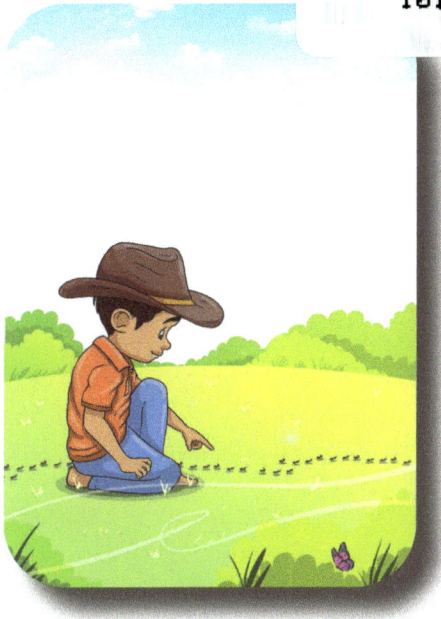

By JBus

Library For All Ltd.

What's This?

We respect and honour Aboriginal and Torres Strait Islander Elders past, present and future. We acknowledge the stories, traditions and living cultures of Aboriginal and Torres Strait Islander peoples on this land and commit to building a brighter future together.

What's this?

It is a black ant.

3

What's this?

It is a buzzing bee.

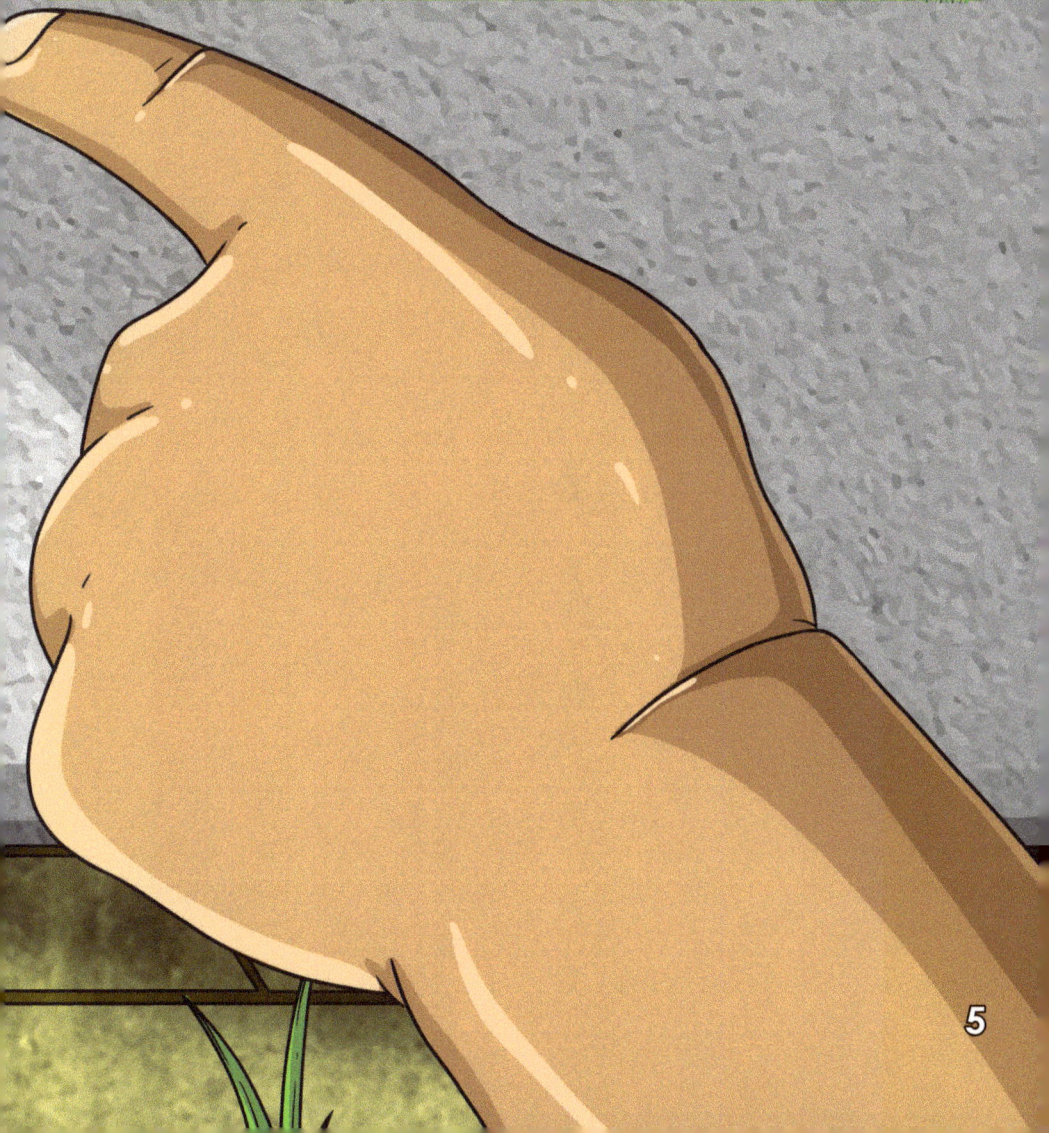

What's this?

It is a flying beetle.

What's this?

It is a small caterpillar.

What's this?

It is a green grasshopper.

What's this?

It is a wiggly worm.

What's this?

It is a leaping lizard.

What's this?

It is a baby bird.

What else can you see in the garden?

Ant

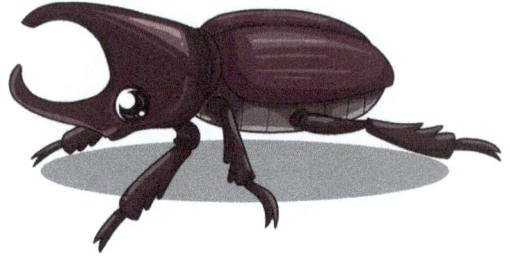

Beetle

Lizard

Worm

Grasshopper   Caterpillar

Bee   Bird

You can use these questions to talk about this book with your family, friends and teachers.

What did you learn from this book?

Describe this book in one word. Funny? Scary? Colourful? Interesting?

How did this book make you feel when you finished reading it?

What was your favourite part of this book?

About the author

JBus is a Kabi Kabi woman from Queensland and lives in Brisbane. She enjoys being at the beach with her family, creating art and singing.

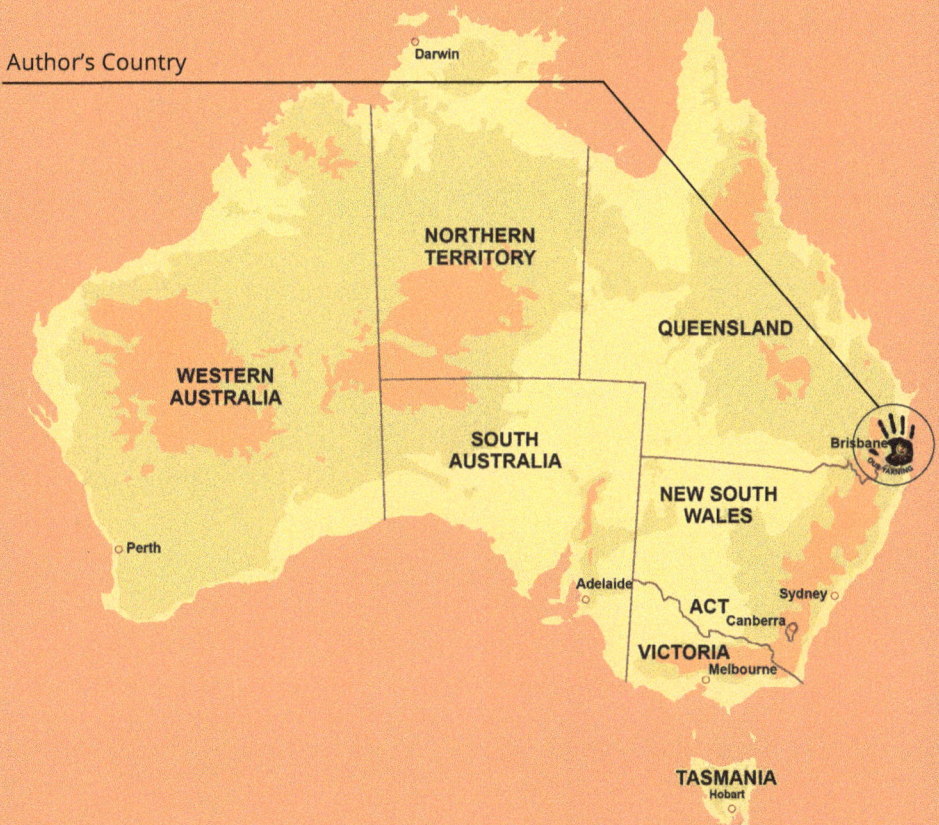

Author's Country

Darwin

NORTHERN
TERRITORY

QUEENSLAND

WESTERN
AUSTRALIA

SOUTH
AUSTRALIA

Brisbane

Perth

NEW SOUTH
WALES

Adelaide

Sydney

ACT
Canberra

VICTORIA
Melbourne

TASMANIA
Hobart

Our Yarning

Want to discover more books from this collection? Our Yarning is a collection of books written by Aboriginal and Torres Strait Islander peoples across Australia.

We know that children learn better, and enjoy reading more, when they see themselves in the stories, characters and illustrations of the books they read.

To download the app, visit the Google Play Store on any Android device and search 'Our Yarning'.

www.ingramcontent.com/pod-product-compliance
Lightning Source LLC
Chambersburg PA
CBHW042349040426
42448CB00019B/3468